Art Created by Melissa LaDue

Meet Me at the Bridge
Copyright © 2024 by Melissa LaDue DBA Written by Mo Jo Jo

All rights reserved.
No part of this book may be copied, shared, or transmitted by any means, whether mechanical, electronic, or otherwise, without prior written consent from the author or publisher. Exceptions are granted only for brief quotations used in reviews or other non-commercial uses permitted by copyright law

Published by Melissa LaDue DBA Written By Mo Jo Jo via Blurb Books

11/14/2024 First Edition ISBN on back cover.

Cover Design: Melissa LaDue/ Interior Design: Melissa LaDue

DISCLAIMER: The poems in this collection are works of creative expression. Any resemblance to actual persons or events is coincidental. AI was used in the creation of this book for images and editing.

For permissions and inquiries, please contact: Melissa LaDue at https://www.writtenbymojojo.com

Meet Me at the Bridge

Poetry Bridging Head and Heart

By Melissa LaDue
dba Written by
Mo Jo Jo

GRATITUDE & ACKNOWLEDGMENTS

This book exists because of the encouragement, compassion, and wisdom of many beautiful souls.
To the creative, spiritual, and entrepreneurial communities who walked with me, sharing inspiration and reminding me that none of us is alone - thank you.

To Adam Roa, Amena Siddiqi, Bridget S., and the mentors, friends, and kindred spirits who offered wisdom and solace - thank you for reminding me that joy and pain are interwoven threads in a full life. To the silent supporters who stood in the background as I sought validation in the wrong places, your quiet presence taught me what true support means.

To Nick - thank you for all you gave me, for the memories, and for amicable understanding in the end. I'm grateful for the time we shared.

To Ben, Charlie, and their dog Wesley - thank you for giving me a warm space to complete this book. Your friendship is a gift.

And to "Mine Muse", a guiding presence who entered my life, fueling this journey in ways I may never fully understand but will always feel - your impact is profound, mysterious, and cherished beyond words.

DEDICATION

To everyone on a healing path, moving through the depths of their own dark nights may this book serve as a light, reminding you of your resilience and boundless capacity to find love, even when the journey feels anything but gentle.

To each person who may one day hold this book in their hands and find a piece of their own story within it - thank you for allowing my words to walk beside you. I may not know how far this book will reach, but if it speaks to even one person who sees themselves in these pages, then every step of this journey was truly worth it.

AUTHOR'S NOTE

Because I chose to live, I wrote this book in the hope that sharing my journey might help light the way for others walking through their own dark times. Life throws some heavy, complex truths our way - moments that test us, break us open, and leave us wondering if we are the only ones just trying to keep it together. But we are not alone. We're all woven together by these shared, messy experiences, even if we can't always see it.

This collection is my attempt to bridge that space between head and heart. It's a gathering of the love I have questioned, the fears I have faced, and the truths I have had to accept, pieced together into poems that invite you to dig deeper into your own story. Each piece and reflection are here to encourage radical honesty, to help you embrace both light and dark, and to remind you that everything you are feeling, everything you are going through - it all matters. It is okay to not be okay; let hope remain, always.

As you read, I hope you find clarity in the reflections and courage in the questions, and maybe even discover that you are not walking this path alone. Live, laugh, love - even when it's tough.

 - Melissa / Mo Jo Jo

TABLE OF CONTENTS

I. Resilience and Growth
Resilient Fire
No Half Measures
The Plunge
Duality in Growth
Frozen in Time
Restless Creation
The Calling
Pressure Cooker
I Cannot Keep Doing This…
Authentically Me
Enough In This Moment

II. Love and Connection
Over-thinking Love
Unworthy of Love
By His Side
Cotton Candy on a Rainy Day
Grateful Hearts
Love Bridge
O Holy Knight
King & Queen Dreams
Arbor Amatis (The Tree You Love)
In This Wonderland of Dreams
Diamonds & Pearls (Glamour & Bliss)

III. Grief and Letting Go

Shattered Bliss
In the Aftermath
Duality in Healing
See You on the Other Side (Then & Now)
Duality in Loss
Gone By Sunrise
Waiting
A Breath of Fresh Air
Letting Go of Yesterday
Picture Perfect
The Space Between Us

IV. Complex Truths

Victim & Witness
Unrequited Love = Mismatched Hearts
The Weight
Bound and Free: A Duality (Bound & Free)
Perception & Deception: The Duality of Beauty
Self-Deception? Shift Perception.
In Silence
Diversity through Unity
Hidden in Plain Sight
The Feather's Weight: A Scribe's Truth
Paradox: Certainty & Doubt

SECTION I.

RESILIENCE AND GROWTH

RESILIENT FIRE

Do not treat me like I'm stupid
Do not treat me like I'm dumb
When I get really angry – I get quiet
And want to bite clean through my tongue.

Do not take advantage of me
Do not tell me lies
I will walk away
I will not hide behind a disguise.

Do not think me selfish
Do not think me unkind
Do not expect me to sacrifice my dreams
If you are not willing to stay by my side.

Do not expect everything from me
Yet deliver me nothing in return
I do not seek your approval
And if needed, in the flames I will burn.

I will follow my path
I will stay true and strong
From the ashes I will rise
Even if it means that I was wrong.

RESILIENT FIRE - REFLECTION

In a world that often demands more than it offers, resilience means choosing your path over the one that others would lay out for you. "Resilient Fire" is about honoring your truth, even if it means walking alone. Setting boundaries is not an act of selfishness but an act of strength - a way of claiming space for your dreams and values.

How does standing up for yourself help you define who you are, even if it means going against the grain? In what ways can resilience allow us to rise, imperfect yet true to ourselves?

READER NOTES:

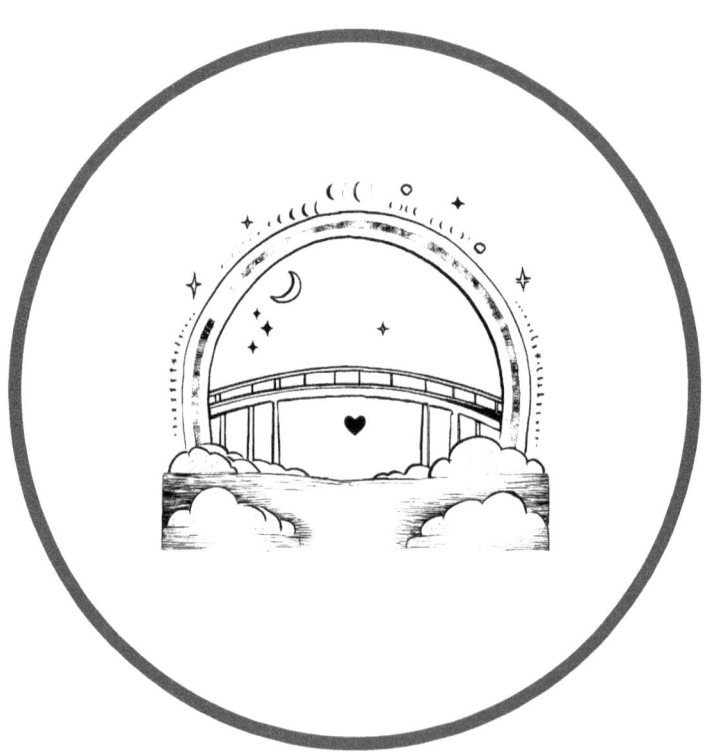

NO HALF MEASURES

I've always gone all in -
half measures don't suffice,
I've felt life's weight too vividly,
seen its cost and price.
When I'm all in, I burn bright;
but when I hold back, it stews,
Dust settles in tidy corners,
yet old wounds break loose.

I thought I'd unpacked enough,
my scattered past laid bare,
but this year, those boxes broke,
spilling shadows everywhere.
Grief and love, they refuse
to be neatly contained,
They find cracks, slip through walls,
till only truth remains.

I once thought resilience
meant keeping it all tight,
Braving each storm without flinching,
no weakness in sight.
But maybe it's letting go -
of half-truths and masked parts,
Daring to fall and rebuild
from the rawest of starts.

Life doesn't leave room
for the fearful or the faint,
It presses, it demands,
with colors both dark and quaint.

So I answer, unguarded, bearing scars,
lessons and grace,
Ready to stumble, to burn, and to rise -
unafraid of this place.

NO HALF MEASURES - REFLECTION

Choosing to live with depth and honesty requires courage; it asks us to face the parts of ourselves we may otherwise keep hidden. "No Half Measures" challenges us to step fully into life, trusting that embracing our scars and vulnerabilities leads to genuine growth. Resilience isn't about perfection; it's about daring to be whole.

How might embracing vulnerability allow you to grow beyond old limitations? In what ways does going all in, even when it's uncomfortable, create space for a truer, more resilient self?

READER NOTES:

THE PLUNGE

What a tangled web we weave
When ourselves we do deceive,
A grave injustice, it is indeed,
When self-honesty is what we need.

At the bridge's rail I stare,
Pondering the weights I bare.
In the reflection, I dare to see,
Could these woven lies still save me?

Or will breaking through them set me free?
Letting go the thoughts of old,
I take the plunge into waters cold,
With trembling hope and courage bold.

To forge my heart into purest gold,
And rise unbroken, fearless, and whole.

THE PLUNGE – REFLECTION

We often hold onto comforting illusions, believing they protect us from pain. But as "The Plunge" suggests, true freedom lies in letting go. Sometimes, breaking through our own barriers is what allows us to grow stronger and more authentic.

What parts of yourself might you be holding back? How can facing your fears help you embrace a truer version of who you are?

READER NOTES:

DUALITY IN GROWTH
HAVE YOU CONSIDERED?

Have you ever considered
what it is like to be
the fruit that hangs
from the branch on a tree?

You start in the spring
a bud breaking through snow
a little water and light
see how you grow.

The seasons they change
they come and go
the weather and birds
taking their toll.

Then the winter sets in,
the cold winds blow...
Fine by the day,
struggle by night,
wondering when
the time will be right...

To let go of the branch
and fall to the ground,
and let the circle restart
with your life in the ground…

DUALITY IN GROWTH
DID YOU CONSIDER?

Did you consider
what it was like to be
the fruit hanging
from the branch on the tree?

The leaves have fallen,
the tree mostly bare,
despite the challenges,
the fruit is still there.

The seasons, they change
in the blink of an eye,
less than 30 days later
the snow falls from the sky.

The winter is setting in,
the cold winds blow...
The fruit has decided
not to let go.
It hangs on for now,
clinging to its tree...

Not letting go,
not falling down,
choosing to keep
its life above ground.

DUALITY IN GROWTH - REFLECTION

Growth often requires us to make difficult choices between holding on and letting go, each demanding its own kind of resilience. "Duality in Growth" speaks to the power of embracing both paths - the strength to endure and the courage to release when the time is right. Recognizing this balance can be a key part of understanding ourselves and moving forward authentically.

How might recognizing the balance between holding on and letting go help you navigate times of change? What has choosing to hold on - or let go - revealed about your own resilience?

READER NOTES:

FROZEN IN TIME

I'm so scared, I can hardly move,
Sunsets on water, fading smooth.
How many more will I get to see?
The light is gone, reflections flee.

I'm running on empty, but still I fight,
I need this moment to feel alive.
The cold November air chills the shore,
The silence is sweet, but I need more.

I can hardly move, frozen inside,
I need someone to turn the tide.
I'm at maximum speed, losing control,
The black forest looms, taking its toll.

I need to come home, but change is in the air,
Things fall apart, and it's my despair.
The sun sets on this lonely life,
So cold, so sharp, cutting like a knife.

FROZEN IN TIME - REFLECTION

Fear can leave us feeling paralyzed, unable to move forward or back. "Frozen in Time" reflects those moments of feeling emotionally stuck, when change is on the horizon but feels just out of reach. It's about the tension between wanting more and being held back by what's familiar.

What steps can we take to break free when fear keeps us frozen? How might the stillness of fear be a signal of an inner desire for change?

READER NOTES:

RESTLESS CREATION

Paint by number,
A new instrument perhaps,
Sudden urge to learn a language,
But then my energy collapsed.

Searching the fog of my restless mind,
Unraveling the mystery within.
Where are those happy, beautiful days,
From before the grief set in?

The canvas is empty, the violin still,
I reach for the thread of something real.
Creativity calls, like a breath of air,
Pulling me close, pulling me there.

I welcome the chaos, the colors, the sound,
In creation, my spirit is found.

RESTLESS CREATION – REFLECTION

Creativity brings hidden thoughts and emotions to life, helping us make sense of what's inside, even when words fall short. "Restless Creation" reflects the pull to create, especially when life feels overwhelming or unclear. Creativity isn't just about making something; it's about finding ourselves in the process.

How can we use creativity to reconnect with parts of ourselves that feel lost? In what ways can embracing our creative urges help us feel more grounded and understood?

READER NOTES:

THE CALLING

I hear thunderous spirits,
But see condemning eyes,
I feel the scales begin to shift,
As the barn owl cries.

Once destructive to the art,
The rift between head and heart,
Now settles softly into place,
A unified world takes its shape.

With wings unfurled,
We find love and grace,
Bathed in cosmic light,
Spanning time and space.

She begins to fly,
She starts to soar,
No longer bound
By chains of yore.

The spirit is called,
No path is wrong or right,
Though futures remain uncertain,
A fire-bird emerges from darkest night.

___

THE CALLING – REFLECTION

Sometimes, growth means breaking away from what's expected and listening to the quiet pull of our own hearts. "The Calling" explores the courage it takes to follow our own truth, even if it means moving away from familiar patterns and paths. It's about the journey toward inner harmony and self-acceptance.

What happens when we forge a new path instead of carrying the burdens of the past? How can listening to our inner voice help us find clarity and purpose?

READER NOTES:

PRESSURE COOKER

Do your best.
Try your hardest.
Be the best.
Failure isn't an option.

Mediocrity isn't good enough.

You could have done better.
It was OK.
You'll do better next time.
Practice makes perfect.
Why didn't you get an A?
Better luck next time.

I can only do so much.
I'm only human.
Get off my back.
I'm sick of all the pressure.

There's no such thing as PERFECT!

PRESSURE COOKER – REFLECTION

We often place immense pressure on ourselves to be "good enough" in a world that constantly demands more. "Pressure Cooker" speaks to the strain of those expectations and the exhaustion that comes from trying to meet impossible standards. True resilience comes from letting go of these pressures and finding value in who we are, flaws and all.

What would happen if you allowed yourself to be "enough" without meeting every expectation? How could releasing some of the pressure help you grow in ways that feel more real and fulfilling?

READER NOTES:

I CANNOT KEEP DOING THIS…

I cannot keep doing this, it's time to move on.
Lost in darkness, singing a sad song.
Telling myself "It will be okay".
Repeating that mantra every single day.

But the truth of the matter is…
I hate feeling this way.
All my heart feels… is pain.
But I keep saying "It will be okay".

I believe in honesty.
I believe in integrity.
I believe in genuine human connection,
And that love conquers all.

I believed in myself.
When no one else did.
I would stay awake for hours.
Thinking about things that I did.

Crying myself to sleep.
Wishing I was dead.
Thinking about things
That other people said.

Recital: "It could have been better."
Future Career: "That's not for you."
2nd Place Award: "You should have tried harder."
I do not like [fill in the blank]: "There's nothing you can do."

But the ones closest to me,
That is what they said.

So, I just closed myself off...
And hid away instead.

Always sinking deeper
Thinking "I am not a keeper."
Foolishly looking for a savior…
Through self-destructive behavior.

"Get up! keep going!"
"It's all in your head."
"It's not that bad."
The pep talks with myself I had.

I never gave in…
I couldn't spread that pain.
I couldn't leave another person,
Crying in the rain.

Constant cycles
On Rinse and Repeat
Highs and lows…
My demons to defeat.

Nearly 20 years later…
I've returned to my craft.
I've found my people.
I'm writing my first novel draft.

I finally found myself again.
Lots of smiles, laughter and picture poses.
And no, it is not -
all rainbows and roses.

I do my best…Day by day.
Life is not a test…It's a journey.

I'm learning to love my mess.
I'm learning to rest.
I'm learning to feel blessed.
When life gives you lemons… learn to zest.

I will keep going.
Words are my song.
I have light and love in my heart.
Finally, this is me…moving on.

I CANNOT KEEP DOING THIS... – REFLECTION

Life can sometimes feel like an endless cycle of doubt and disappointment. "I Cannot Keep Doing This..." speaks to the courage it takes to finally say "enough." In a world of imposed ideals, self-acceptance becomes a radical act of resilience, allowing us to break free from unhelpful patterns. Recognizing and embracing these cycles can be a powerful step toward clarity and growth.

How can self-acceptance help you recognize and confront the patterns that no longer serve you? What small steps might allow you to embrace your true self and find freedom in the journey?

READER NOTES:

AUTHENTICALLY ME

Dancing to and fro
Between shadow and light
You are not alone
If this is your fight

Despair is a disease
So, hold your heart tight
You might find yourself torn
Between wrong and right

Wondering what are the lies
And what will be revealed with true sight
It's okay to guard your heart
Hold safe that which brings you delight

You may feel lost and alone
Like you can't win this fight
Like all you have are scars and pain
And even drawing breath is a blight

I beg you to remain in this life
Please know, one day, it will be alright
Even if you feel like no one cares
There is at least one that sees your light

Someone who cares for you.
You're thinking:
How do you know?

Right?
Because, I was once that someone
For one who lost their fight.

They didn't know
They couldn't see
They lost all hope
They lost to their disease

And in losing THEM
I almost lost ME

So, no matter what
Hold your heart tight
Have hope and guard it well
Cherish every delight

Move forward one day at a time
Let them see your beautiful light.

AUTHENTICALLY ME – REFLECTION

In times of struggle, it's easy to feel like our light doesn't matter. "Authentically Me" reminds us that even in the darkest moments, holding onto our inner light is an act of resilience. It's about finding strength in self-compassion and recognizing that our presence has meaning, not only for ourselves but for others who may need us.

When life feels overwhelming, what small steps can help you reconnect with your inner light? How can you nurture yourself in a way that reminds you of your worth?

READER NOTES:

ENOUGH IN THIS MOMENT

Time drifts like clouds across the sky,
I sit beneath, no need to try.
In this stillness, I find my way,
Where I am is enough today.

Love me or hate me, take me or leave,
I stand as I am, and I believe,
In every flaw, every scar, every line,
This heart, this soul, they're wholly mine.

I've learned I'm enough, as the waves crash down,
As I stand on the brink, where fears nearly drown.
In the quiet, I see my own worth take shape,
Not bound by others, free to escape.

As long as I love myself, with all my curves and bends,
I can climb each ledge, make amends.
This journey of growth is steady, not fast,
A love for myself that's built to last.

No need for masks, no need to pretend,
With each step forward, old doubts mend.
In this moment, I am whole, complete,
Enough as I am, on my own two feet.

ENOUGH IN THIS MOMENT - REFLECTION

Self-acceptance is an act of resilience, one that allows us to find peace with who we are, regardless of others' opinions. "Enough In This Moment" is about trusting in our own worth and finding strength in simply being present. True growth often lies in realizing that we are enough as we are, even if the journey is ongoing.

How might embracing who you are right now free you from the expectations of others? In what ways can self-acceptance create a foundation for future growth?

READER NOTES:

SECTION II.

<u>LOVE AND CONNECTION</u>

OVER-THINKING LOVE

Whirling thoughts inside my head,
Not sure what to feel or where to tread.
It's raining, and I'm stuck in place,
Longing for love's gentle embrace.

I analyze each word, each look, each sound,
In love's maze, I keep spinning around.
The seasons change, but love, I fear,
Shouldn't it last, year after year?

Raindrops fall, like thoughts in a storm,
Each one different, each a new form.
I wish for peace, for love to just be,
Not trapped by the questions inside of me.

OVER-THINKING LOVE – REFLECTION

In our efforts to understand love, we sometimes lose sight of its simplicity and beauty. "Over-thinking Love" speaks to the tendency to dissect every word, look, and gesture, trapping ourselves in a cycle of doubt. Love, like rain, flows naturally, and trying to control it can often lead to unnecessary turmoil.

How can releasing the need to analyze help us experience love more freely? What would it look like to let love just to be, without trying to define or question every aspect?

READER NOTES:

UNWORTHY OF LOVE

I'm unworthy of their love,
Though I cannot say why,
I love them so deeply,
Yet can't speak, just cry.

My light is fading,
I can't reach their hand,
My heart's not meant for theirs,
But I don't understand.

I lie here dying,
Will they ever be mine?
Or will I be left alone,
Counting tears in time?

Will I end up in darkness,
With no one by my side,
Sit and mourn the love I lost,
Because I wasn't worthy inside?

UNWORTHY OF LOVE – REFLECTION

When we feel unworthy, love can seem like a distant dream, something meant for others but out of reach for us. "Unworthy of Love" speaks to the quiet heartache of wanting connection while doubting we deserve it. Learning to see ourselves as worthy of love requires us to confront these fears and insecurities, to nurture self-compassion and acceptance.

How can we learn to embrace ourselves, flaws and all, and open our hearts to the love we desire? What small steps might allow us to release feelings of unworthiness and build a foundation of self-acceptance?

READER NOTES:

BY HIS SIDE

My hero is different,
A hero of the heart,
Strong and gentle,
Compassionate from the start.

I stand by his side,
Though he may not know,
He's there for me too,
When my pain doesn't show.

He doesn't know,
That I'm slowly dying,
I try to tell him,
But it feels like I'm lying.

No words will come,
When I need them the most,
So, I leave him unaware,
Letting him choose his post.

BY HIS SIDE – REFLECTION

Sometimes, love means holding space for someone even when we feel unseen ourselves. "By His Side" captures the silent courage it takes to support others while carrying our own pain. True connection doesn't always require words; sometimes, it's found in simply being present for each other, even through unspoken struggles.

What fears keep us from opening up to those we love? How might embracing vulnerability bring us closer and deepen the bonds we share?

READER NOTES:

COTTON CANDY ON A RAINY DAY

A vision of light,
In my darkest hour,
My pillar, my strength,
My guiding tower.

Lover of lovers,
Friend of friends,
The glue that binds
The fragmented ends.

The usual fears,
No longer linger here,
Your light pierced my dark,
The shadows disappear.

No light shines brighter,
No comfort more true,
The pain fades away,
In the warmth of you.

No words can explain
The feelings I display,
Or why I hold this cotton candy
On a rainy day.

COTTON CANDY ON A RAINY DAY – REFLECTION

In life's darkest moments, the simplest acts of love can be our strongest source of light. "Cotton Candy on a Rainy Day" speaks to the beauty of finding comfort and joy in unexpected places, especially when shared with someone who truly sees us. Love doesn't always come with grand gestures; sometimes, it's the quiet presence that turns rain into something sweet.

How can the simple presence of another bring warmth when shadows linger? How do we find small, precious moments of sweetness amidst life's storms, allowing love to be our guide?

READER NOTES:

GRATEFUL HEARTS

Fluffing your hair with both hands
Planting kisses on your forehead
Your cheeks
Your nose
Your chin
Then finally, your lips I seek.

Holding each other tight
Time
Slips
Silent
Into the night.

No space between our bodies
Chests pressed together
Fingers interlaced
Hearts beating as one
Breathing in unison
We come undone.

Two halves meet
A new year to greet
Together
Forever

The lovers coo
Mine
Eternity
With you.

Lovers united
Under the falling snow
Grateful hearts
Wrapped up with a bow.

GRATEFUL HEARTS – REFLECTION

True love often reveals itself in the quiet moments - the shared laughter, the gentle touch, the silent understanding between two hearts. "Grateful Hearts" reminds us that it's these simple, genuine connections that bring lasting joy and fulfillment. When we learn to appreciate these small, beautiful instances, we nurture a deeper bond that transcends the superficial.

How can gratitude for these moments enhance the love we share with others? In what ways can we learn to treasure the everyday experiences that build a foundation of connection?

READER NOTES:

LOVE BRIDGE

To be honest, to be grateful
To be humble, to be kind
To be strong, to be faithful
To be seen by the blind
To be smart, to be true
To see the real in you.

To meet in the middle
To solve your heart's riddle
To let you come inside
The walls where I reside.

To see where your heart hides
To see the love inside your eyes
To discern the truth behind the lies
To take things in stride
To leave the old behind.

To grow closer across time
 No distance can subside
A connection sublime
 This is what I know
When you call me "mine".

LOVE BRIDGE – REFLECTION

"Love Bridge" speaks to the strength required to open our hearts and meet someone halfway, allowing trust and vulnerability to guide us forward. True love is about embracing the full scope of who we are, while daring to solve the riddles of our hearts together.

What does it mean to let someone past your guard, to meet them across the bridge of vulnerability? How can we learn to approach love as a journey of shared growth and mutual understanding?

READER NOTES:

O HOLY KNIGHT

On this glorious night,
I look towards the heavens,
I bathe in moonlight.

I am at peace with myself.
My soul feels… right.

I am the sky and the sky is me.
The Eastern star shines for all to see.

I am grace and I am sunshine.
O Holy Knight…thank you for rescuing me.
O Holy Knight…. Thank you, for being Mine.
As the world continues to turn… I am fine.

O HOLY KNIGHT - REFLECTION

"O Holy Knight" speaks to the deep gratitude we feel when someone or something brings us back to ourselves during dark times. This light, whether from within, another person, or a higher power, grounds us, offering peace and hope.

How can finding that inner or outer "knight" help us feel grateful for moments of rescue and renewal? In what ways does gratitude for these experiences strengthen our resolve to keep moving forward?

READER NOTES:

KING & QUEEN DREAMS

He stood magnificently on the silver screen,
The lone viewer of the night was the Red Queen.
He broke the fourth wall… and handed her a bronze ring.
They joined hands and began to dance and sing.
I give you my heart and soul… she said to her Winter King…

All the while, their love grew,
They drank each other in like morning dew.
Despite all odds, their love was true.
They chased sunrise from their sunset hue.
He was the muse of her heart, and King of her night,
The Queen vanquished his darkness. with her brilliant light.

The King and Queen shared such a simple dream,
And it was not to live life trying to be unseen.
They wanted a simple and blissful, glamorous life.
To have and to hold, he would make her his wife.
Travel the world, support each other's dreams,
While raising two lovely girls, so it seems.
Planning to grow a garden and flowers every spring.
Oh! What joy this will bring!

They enjoyed chocolate-covered strawberries,
And shared in champagne dreams.
My Blissful Luxury!
Now, THAT sets the scene.

Two lovers we find…
They are very keen…
Entangled in sheets…
The King kisses his Queen.

Now! Wake UP! Happy New Year!
He was gone, but she held no fear.
He was safely where she left him, on his silver screen.
Now, wasn't that a wonderful dream?
Is that the end…
Or are these just the initial scenes…
In this epic tale of a King and Queen…
That began with their dreams within dreams…?

KING & QUEEN DREAMS – REFLECTION

True love transcends time, form, and even reality, existing as much in dreams as in waking moments. "King & Queen Dreams" invites us into a fairytale world, where love defies limits and lives on, even if only within our imagination.

How do our dreams shape our hopes for real-life connections? In what ways can allowing ourselves to dream bring a sense of joy and fulfillment, even if the dream exists only within our hearts?

READER NOTES:

ARBOR AMATIS
(LATIN FOR "THE TREE OF LOVE")

My tree wants to be
Something else entirely
But the gods made it just for me
My love, reincarnated as a tree
Tall and strong, Beautiful and green
The soul is there, in truth, I've seen

Beneath its branches I will rest,
Whilst I daydream of my lover's quest
Flowers I will plant in the spring
In the summer I will decorate it with colored string
Wreathes I will fashion from its fallen leaves
Wrap it in straw to prevent a winter freeze

I will give it water and sunlight to grow
It will shelter me as the storms blow
And when it's time for me to finally go
They can wrap me up in a shroud apropos
And at its roots they can plant me
Beneath my beloved tree
It can then feed from me
Two souls now bound, eternally.

ARBOR AMATIS - REFLECTION

"Arbor Amatis" explores a love that defies time and form - a soulmate reincarnated as a tree, symbolizing an eternal bond that endures beyond the physical. This devotion transcends the usual boundaries, nurturing a connection that grows and evolves, even in unexpected forms. It speaks to love as a force that continues to protect and unify, suggesting that true love reaches beyond traditional limits.

How can we nurture love in ways that go beyond conventional expectations? In what ways does the idea of being eternally connected provide comfort and purpose?

READER NOTES:

IN THIS WONDERLAND OF DREAMS

In this wonderland where dreams entwine,
Our souls embrace beyond all time.
Beneath the stars, a world we share,
A whispered love beyond compare.

Your voice, a melody on air,
Your touch, a warmth that lingers there.
Here, in the stillness, we are free,
To dance beneath eternity.

But as the moon begins to fade,
A shadowed fear begins to wade.
What if this dream is all we'll know?
Will morning light force us to go?

Yet still, I hold this dream so near,
A place untouched by time or fear.
For in this wonderland, we're one,
A love unbroken, never undone.

DIAMONDS & PEARLS
(GLAMOUR & BLISS)

Fame. Fortune. Luxury. Glamour. Bliss.
Are all of those words... synonymous?
Without all of them, will life be amiss?
Do they all bring... true happiness?

Fame. Fortune. Luxury.
All the perceived glitz and glam...
Will that bring your heart joy?
Or make it close up like a clam?

Textbook definitions of glamour and bliss:
That's true happiness to me...
It's like art and beauty...
In the eye of the beholder... that's where you'll see...

Glamour and bliss...
True love and happiness... without a doubt...
Come from the simplest of things...
That once are found, we can't live without...

Comforting hugs, gifts made by hand...
Quiet nights in, exciting dates planned...
Making a meal together...
just enjoying the weather.

Taking a walk in the park...
having conversations in the dark.

It's in the magic you feel...
by just holding hands...
Or finding out you like
the same types of movies and bands.
It's in hearing the laughter,
seeing the smiles that you miss...
Receiving a cute photo from your sweetie...
that makes you send back a kiss...

It's not about fame,
or fortune, or a life of luxury...
That's not what I want or miss...

It's the enchantment and happiness
found together...
That's how I define...
glamour and bliss.

DIAMONDS & PEARLS - REFLECTION

True glamour and bliss often lie in life's simplest moments, beyond the allure of fame or fortune. "Diamonds & Pearls (Glamour & Bliss)" reminds us that real happiness is found in shared laughter, quiet companionship, and the magic of connection. By returning to the heart of what brings us joy, we uncover a truth that endures beyond material pursuits.

What small, everyday moments bring true glamour into your life? How can embracing simplicity deepen your sense of fulfillment?

READER NOTES:

SHATTERED BLISS - REFLECTION

"Shattered Bliss" captures the grief of releasing comforting illusions and facing deeper truths. Sometimes, healing starts when we let go of the versions of ourselves or our lives that felt easier but ultimately held us back. This poem reflects the discomfort of that first step toward self-awareness - a necessary shift that's both painful and transformative.

How does confronting uncomfortable truths pave the way for growth? In what ways can letting go of illusions open us to a more authentic life? What moments of "shattered bliss" have led you to reevaluate your path?

READER NOTES:

IN THE AFTERMATH

The beautiful bright light,
In your shining eyes,
Is more precious to me
Than all the stars in the sky.

Your childlike grin
Brings a smile every time
And stops the sad flow
Of these tears of mine.

When the hues change
From vivid color to dull gray,
I'll be there for you
Each night and every day.

A shoulder to cry on,
A hand to squeeze,
When you think you can't win
And you fall to your knees.

You're never alone
Against the demons you face,
I'll always be there for you
Throughout all time and space.

IN THE AFTERMATH – REFLECTION

Grief takes many forms, but nothing prepares you for the pain of losing someone who once pulled you from the depths. "In the Aftermath" speaks to the sorrow and lingering questions that arise when we lose a loved one who once offered us strength. This poem is both a tribute and a reminder of the quiet impact that love and friendship leave behind. In grieving, we may also carry a lost opportunity to have offered the same lifeline they extended to us.

How can we honor those we've lost by carrying forward the love they gave us? In what ways can grief remind us of the importance of being present for others, even in subtle ways? What would it look like to turn survivor's guilt into a tribute, using it as a guide to support others in need?

READER NOTES:

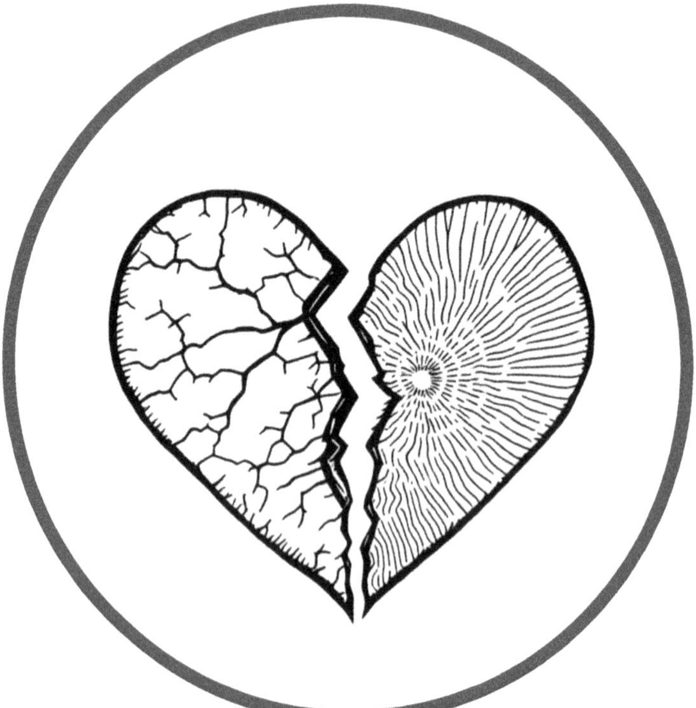

DUALITY IN HEALING: NOW
MENDED EFFECTS Written 11/12/2023

...I stood broken and beaten
... Bleeding in the rain
...But I did not give up
... Despite the pain.

...The dream was dead
... Dormant and cold
... It was given a gift
...A story to unfold.

...From damaged goods
...Came mended effects
... From a wounded heart
... Only love collects.

...Berry Lips
...Hazel Eyes
...A beautiful soul
... Needs no disguise.

...Desired
...Adored
...Happy and Free
...Mended beyond compare.

...Mended Effects
...Baggage Stowed
...Unforgotten graves
...The hill is hallowed.

...The hole in my heart
...Sewn and sealed
...Happy and whole
...With time was healed.

...Reaching out
...Found a hand to hold
...A shoulder to cry on
...A love to be bold.

...These mended effects
...Sheltered from the rain
...Happy and whole
...Feeling no pain.

DUALITY IN HEALING – REFLECTION

"Duality in Healing" is a journey through the layers of trauma and resilience - first through "Damaged Goods," which reflects the weight of unprocessed pain, and then with "Mended Effects," capturing the gradual acceptance and healing that follow. These poems illustrate the complex path from recognizing deep wounds to redefining oneself beyond them. Healing doesn't erase what happened, but it allows us to reclaim a sense of wholeness, integrating past pain as part of our strength.

How can acknowledging the scars we carry help us move toward healing? In what ways does accepting our past shape a more resilient, empowered present? What steps can you take to view yourself as both healed and whole, even when the memories linger?

READER NOTES:

SEE YOU ON THE OTHER SIDE
(THEN) Written 4/16/1999

The tears fall from colored eyes,
With weeping hearts and mournful sighs.
The question I keep asking is "why?"

There is no fault.
There is no blame.
Only tears. Only pain.
We did what we could.
He did what he would.

No way to tell...
To foresee or prevent.
But the pain felt now,
We'll never forget.
They're the hardest to lose,
Those who think they're alone.

Now he has no regrets,
He could never have known
The tears we shed today,
And from here on too,
Are not tears of disappointment,
But tears of love.

Not only have we lost
A brother and son,
But a very dear friend
We will always love.

The tears drop from colored eyes,
With weeping hearts and mournful sighs.
We will love you forever,
As love never dies.

SEE YOU ON THE OTHER SIDE
(NOW) Written 11/11/2023

Lately I've been missing you,
I went to visit your grave,
Most of your family is now with you,
Only your dad remains.

I miss your smile,
I miss your laugh,
I miss my friend,
And the plans we had.

You cut your life short.
I hated you for that.
I collapsed at your funeral,
You were such a brat!

You were not the only one
Who left me behind...
I thought about joining you...
But to others, I could not extend that pain...

Because of that fact,
It seems I have found...
There is more to this life…

More to see, more to feel,
More to be had,
In this life above the ground.

IN THIS WONDERLAND OF DREAMS - REFLECTION

"In This Wonderland of Dreams" invites us into a world where love feels boundless and free from the constraints of time and distance. It reflects the yearning to hold onto a connection that feels as real as it is fragile. The poem speaks to the beauty and vulnerability of dreaming a love that transcends waking life, even as we wonder if it will endure.

How do we cherish these fleeting moments without letting fear overshadow them? What can dreams of love teach us about the connections we seek in the waking world?

READER NOTES:

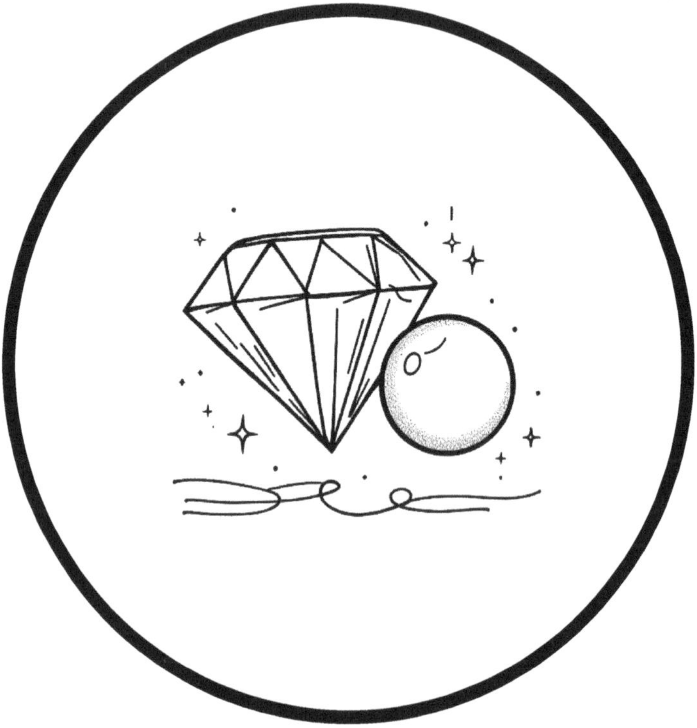

SECTION III.

GRIEF AND LETTING GO

SHATTERED BLISS

So many thoughts
Spinning in my mind
Who the hell am I?

So many years
Wasted in ignorant bliss
Pretending it's a world
That doesn't really exist.

Scared to keep on moving
Of taking on priorities
Living in the real world...
When will I change me?

DUALITY IN HEALING: THEN
DAMAGED GOODS Written 4/15/2008

I stand broken and beaten...
Bleeding in the rain...
Tired of fighting...
Tired of suppressing the pain.

See the cuts...
Watch them bleed...
Soft and quiet...
Like wind through the reeds.

I hide behind...
This painted face...
Hoping to hide...
Without a trace.

Berry Lips...
Hazel Eyes...
Tears well up...
Breaking the disguise.

Unwanted...
Unloved...
Lonely and scared...
Broken beyond repair.

Damaged goods...
Baggage still...
Unforgotten graves...
Up on the hill.

Hole in my heart...
Stomped and torn...
Quiet and broken...
Left forlorn.

Reaching out...
For a hand to hold...
A shoulder to cry on...
A love to be bold.

These damaged goods...
Left in pain...
Broken, beaten...
Dying in the rain.

DUALITY IN HEALING: THEN
DAMAGED GOODS Written 4/15/2008

I stand broken and beaten...
Bleeding in the rain...
Tired of fighting...
Tired of suppressing the pain.

See the cuts...
Watch them bleed...
Soft and quiet...
Like wind through the reeds.

I hide behind...
This painted face...
Hoping to hide...
Without a trace.

Berry Lips...
Hazel Eyes...
Tears well up...
Breaking the disguise.

Unwanted...
Unloved...
Lonely and scared...
Broken beyond repair.

Damaged goods...
Baggage still...
Unforgotten graves...
Up on the hill.

Hole in my heart...
Stomped and torn...
Quiet and broken...
Left forlorn.

Reaching out...
For a hand to hold...
A shoulder to cry on...
A love to be bold.

These damaged goods...
Left in pain...
Broken, beaten...
Dying in the rain.

SEE YOU ON THE OTHER SIDE – REFLECTION

Grief is a journey that changes with time, as captured in "See You on the Other Side (Then & Now)." The first part speaks to the initial shock and sorrow, while the second part reflects a quieter, enduring ache that remains years later. Love and memory keep those we've lost close, even as we learn to live with the absence. Grief doesn't disappear; it evolves, shaping us and teaching us how to move forward while carrying their memory.

How does grief evolve over time, and how can this transformation help us grow? In what ways does honoring our grief allow us to still be connected to those we have lost? How might we channel the love we still hold into actions that keep their spirit alive in our lives?

READER NOTES:

DUALITY IN LOSS
A GLIMPSE OF YOUR FACE

Is it wrong to still want to see
A glimpse of your face?
So many years have passed,
But I still cry tears in this place.

The way the sun glittered
On your color-of-the-month hair,
The way you swept it back
Gently, behind your ear.

Riding bikes in the summer,
Playing games at camp,
Singing songs at the top of our lungs,
Squishing our toes in muddy sand,
Playing with cats.

Not my twin sister,
But you might as well have been that.
We grew apart before we knew it.
So much time had passed.

We became different people,
And swam in different pools,
Only connected by memories shared,
And the laughter of young fools.

Was it something I lacked?
If it hadn't been for that ill-fated crash,
Would we have joined back up for a birthday bash?
It's too late to know… I had to let it go.

You stay in my memories, muddled in my dreams.
It's been 21 years and 1 week since you died at the scene.
And all I still want is to see a glimpse of your face
In my memories of you.

DUALITY IN LOSS
THE MISSED EMBRACE

I watched us drift like leaves on the tide,
Wishing I could have reached you before the storm.
We grew up, grew apart - different paths, different skies,
Yet still, I thought someday we'd find our way back,
reborn.

I kept waiting for that perfect chance,
To take the leap, to give it one more dance.
But distance widened, like shadows at dusk,
Until tragedy took you, leaving us lost, unasked.

I've replayed it countless times,
Imagining your smile when you'd see me again.
Would we laugh, let the past slip into rhyme,
And let our hearts mend, softening the pain?

But fate took the choice from my hand,
A moment of carelessness erased our plans.
I stand here today, a little too late,
With a yearning I cannot satiate.

Now, it's only the whispers of your name,
In old stories shared, a glimpse of your flame.
If I had one more moment, I know what I'd say-
I'd hold you tight, and never let you slip away.

DUALITY IN LOSS – REFLECTION

Losing someone we hoped to reconnect with leaves us with both cherished memories and lingering regrets. In "Duality in Loss", "A Glimpse of Your Face" reflects on joyful moments shared, while "The Missed Embrace" speaks to the pain of missed chances. These poems remind us that, while life often offers second chances, death's finality brings a unique form of grief - a blend of love and longing.

How might we learn to accept the past, even with its unresolved threads? In what ways can acknowledging both joy and regret help us heal? How can we find peace in honoring what was, even when a second chance is no longer possible?

READER NOTES:

GONE BY SUNRISE

Sleeping so sound
I delightfully found
A voice was gently humming

While walking around
In darkness I found
A face was brightly smiling

Writhing without sound
I felt I was bound
by a hand lightly caressing

But I woke on the ground
Alone I was found
Ever so slightly crying

The ghost of you
and all you do
lingers on my skin like lightning

I must redefine
The space and time
For my ghost that vanishes by morning.

GONE BY SUNRISE - REFLECTION

Some connections enter our lives briefly, like a dream that fades by morning, leaving a haunting beauty in their wake. "Gone by Sunrise" reflects the longing for something real yet unattainable - a love or friendship that feels profoundly true, even if it's only a memory or a fleeting presence. This poem explores the poignant experience of temporary bonds that bring comfort, joy, and perhaps a touch of sadness as they vanish with the dawn.

How can we find meaning in connections that don't last? In what ways do these transient encounters shape our understanding of love and companionship? How might embracing these ephemeral moments help us appreciate the beauty of impermanence?

READER NOTES:

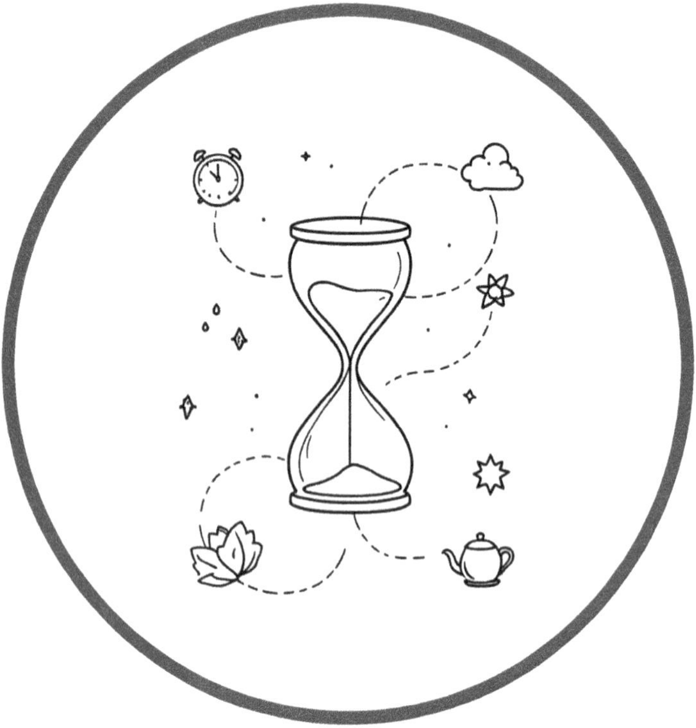

GONE BY SUNRISE - REFLECTION

Some connections enter our lives briefly, like a dream that fades by morning, leaving a haunting beauty in their wake. "Gone by Sunrise" reflects the longing for something real yet unattainable - a love or friendship that feels profoundly true, even if it's only a memory or a fleeting presence. This poem explores the poignant experience of temporary bonds that bring comfort, joy, and perhaps a touch of sadness as they vanish with the dawn.

How can we find meaning in connections that don't last? In what ways do these transient encounters shape our understanding of love and companionship? How might embracing these ephemeral moments help us appreciate the beauty of impermanence?

READER NOTES:

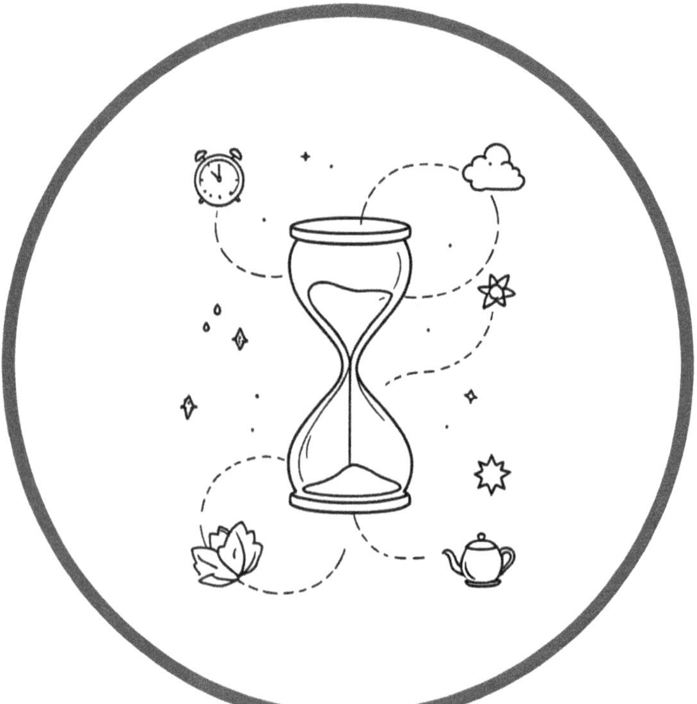

WAITING

This...

Waiting, Waiting, Waiting...

Waiting for trains, planes and cars that go.
Waiting for rains to water the things we grow.
Waiting for the line to move – to get a new shiny thing.
Waiting for the blossoms of spring.
Waiting for traffic lights at night.
Waiting for a thousand stars to show us their light.

Waiting for Guffman, **Waiting** for Godot...
Waiting for the curtain call of tonight's show.
Waiting for love, **Waiting** for peace...
Waiting for the prattling to cease.

Waiting for sunny days.
Waiting for the beans to grind, or tea to steep.
Waiting for the rewards you hope to reap.
Waiting for a raise.
Waiting for a break in the haze.

Always **Waiting**...**Waiting**... **Waiting**...
Waiting... with bated breath... just **waiting**...

Waiting for the time to be right.
Waiting for you to come home at night.
Waiting for water to boil.
Waiting for a refill on heating oil.
Waiting for this, and **Waiting** for that.
Waiting for someone to eat their hat.

Waiting for outcomes to be benign.
Waiting for all **Time**…**waiting** for a sign.
Waiting for someone to toe the line.
Waiting for something to turn out fine.
Waiting for someone's text.
Waiting for what comes next.

Always **Waiting**…. Aggravating.
This…**Waiting, Waiting, Waiting**.

STOP WAITING!

WAITING - REFLECTION

"Waiting" speaks to the moments we spend in anticipation, hoping for things to change, fall into place, or simply arrive. From the mundane to the meaningful, each pause in life can feel like a weight we carry, drawing out our impatience and sometimes our frustration. But there's a turning point - a choice to stop waiting and start living, to embrace what's within reach rather than always looking ahead.

How can we learn to be present even in times of waiting? What might we discover about ourselves if we shift from anticipation to acceptance? In what ways can letting go of the need for control bring more peace to our lives, even as we wait?

READER NOTES:

A BREATH OF FRESH AIR

I chose to live, but not to thrive
My heart was too scarred
I chose to hide

I guarded the tiny ember
That stayed deep in my heart
Hoping and praying
That last bit of warmth would not part

I chose the path of least regret
Knowing full well what was at stake.

Now I ask for freedom,
I ask for space
I ask for life,
A breath of fresh air.

A BREATH OF FRESH AIR - REFLECTION

Comfort can quietly shift into confinement. "A Breath of Fresh Air" captures the moment we see that the walls once built for safety have begun to close us in. The poem speaks to a turning point where survival gives way to a desire for something truer and more aligned with who we are meant to be. Releasing these old forms of safety becomes the first step toward reclaiming freedom.

What protective walls have you built that no longer serve you? How does the idea of "breathing fresh air" shift your view on what you truly need? Where in your life could embracing change lead to freedom?

READER NOTES:

LETTING GO OF YESTERDAY

I once held tight to hidden pain,
A weight that bound like rusted chain.
Old wounds buried, kept close to chest,
Their whispers stealing my chance to rest.

Forgiving others, I'd learned that part,
To free them gently from my heart.
Yet remnants lingered, silent, deep,
In shadows where old grudges sleep.

But forgiving myself seemed a distant shore,
A quiet place I'd long ignored.
Bit by bit, I learned release,
And found in letting go, an inner peace.

I traced each scar, each quiet ache,
And saw the strength those trials did make.
No longer bound to shadows past,
I found a freedom built to last.

Today, I stand in softer light,
Released from chains, unbound, upright.
With every breath, I've come to know -
Healing's a journey, a with an ebb and flow.

LETTING GO OF YESTERDAY - REFLECTION

"Letting Go of Yesterday" touches on the layered process of forgiveness needed to heal past pains. Often, we begin by releasing others, yet the more challenging step is finding self-forgiveness - a journey that requires both patience and compassion. True healing invites us to gradually unbind from yesterday's shadows, allowing us to step into a lighter, freer today.

What past burdens have you released, and what role has forgiveness - both of others and yourself - played in that process? How might embracing self-forgiveness open a path to more freedom in the present? What would it feel like to live fully in today's light, unbound by yesterday's weight?

READER NOTES:

PICTURE PERFECT

A picture-perfect romance,
Yet none of it holds true.
Reflective only on the surface,
In shades of sparkling hues.

>Real love is messy,
>Imperfect, yet profound.
>It's in arguments and hard truths,
>In growth, where healing is found.

Love itself is boundless,
But relationships have lines -
Boundaries and buried triggers,
Weathering both lows and highs.

>Letting go of ideals,
>Of limits, and restraint,
>The fantasy of flawless love -
>An image that can taint.

Real love is tangled,
Both laughter and regret,
Moments of joy and sorrow,
A truth we can't forget.

>The real picture we paint -
>Trust, faith, and imperfect grace -
>Needs space for flaws and freedom,
>For real love's rightful place.

PICTURE PERFECT - REFLECTION

We often grow up with idealized versions of love - images of perfection - polished, flawless, and deceptively simple. "Picture Perfect" challenges the illusion of a neat, fairytale romance and instead embraces the messy, imperfect nature of love. It reminds us that authentic connection comes with difficult conversations, growth, and mutual respect. When we release love from constraints and ideals, we create space for trust and grace that allow relationships to thrive, even through challenges.

How can letting go of the need for "perfect" love deepen our relationships? In what ways might we cultivate love that leaves room for both joy and discomfort, honesty and vulnerability?

READER NOTES:

THE SPACE BETWEEN US

There's a quiet space where you used to be,
A hollow place filled with memory.
I find you there in the in-betweens -
In sunset hues, in morning's sheen.

I miss you most in the simple things,
The laughter shared, the joy it brings.
In silence, I hear echoes clear,
Reminders that you're always here.

Though time moves on, unchanged, unfazed,
And life continues, calmly amazed,
I carry you with each step I take,
A presence gentle, a bittersweet ache.

So here, in this quiet place we've made,
I cherish what will never fade.
Though loss carved out a sacred space,
Love still fills it, like a soft embrace.

THE SPACE BETWEEN US - REFLECTION

Loss often carves out a lasting space, reminding us of the love that endures as we continue forward. "The Space Between Us" touches on the delicate balance of honoring both memory and the quiet absence left by a loved one. This bittersweet ache weaves itself into our days, becoming a part of us and guiding us toward compassion for ourselves as we heal.

What memories have you carried forward, and how have they shaped your path? How might honoring both love and sorrow deepen your connection to yourself and those you've lost? In what ways could acknowledging this space between past and present bring you closer to peace?

READER NOTES:

SECTION IV.

COMPLEX TRUTHS

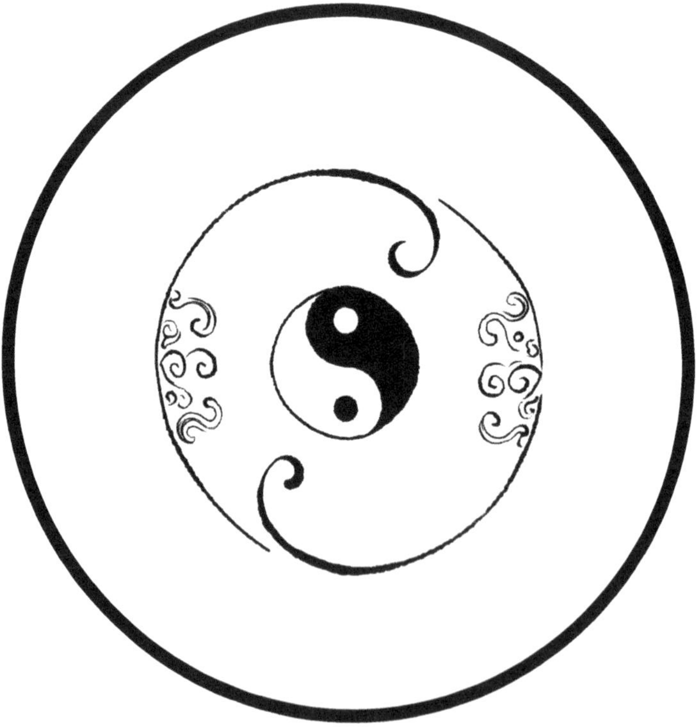

VICTIM & WITNESS

I've been cheated on,
I've been cheated with,
I've been left bruised,
I've been victimized.
I've heard the lies…
Of a love fleeting and intense.

And I've borne witness…

Hotel life,
Spouses on the road,
Men, mostly, those scoundrels…
Their wives and partners,
Asking me questions I can't answer,
While I manage the front-desk phone.
The stories heard while tending bar.
The secret meetings in the car.

The unsuspecting women,
Flirting with men they barely know
This one is Tuesdays,
That one is Thursdays…

Asks me how to tell his wife…
That he's not playing the field…
"Deactivate my old key and give me one new?"
"That girl took my spare and that just won't do…"

Rolling my eyes…
I get it… I do…

Those other women…
They have no clue.
These abhorrent excuses for men…
Their lies seem so true…

I'd be a hypocrite…
If I judged her too…
Having been in that position, it's true…
More than once… I fell for "that line" too.

VICTIM & WITNESS - REFLECTION

"Victim & Witness" reflects the complex position of experiencing betrayal firsthand and then seeing it happen to others. This poem reveals the weight of being both participant and observer, where past pain deepens empathy yet can also blur the line between compassion and judgment. It reminds us that many of life's hardest lessons are shared struggles, connecting us even when we can't intervene or fix the situation.

How can we honor our past pain while recognizing others' vulnerabilities without judgment? What might it mean to grow in empathy by understanding both the victim and witness roles in our own life experiences?

READER NOTES:

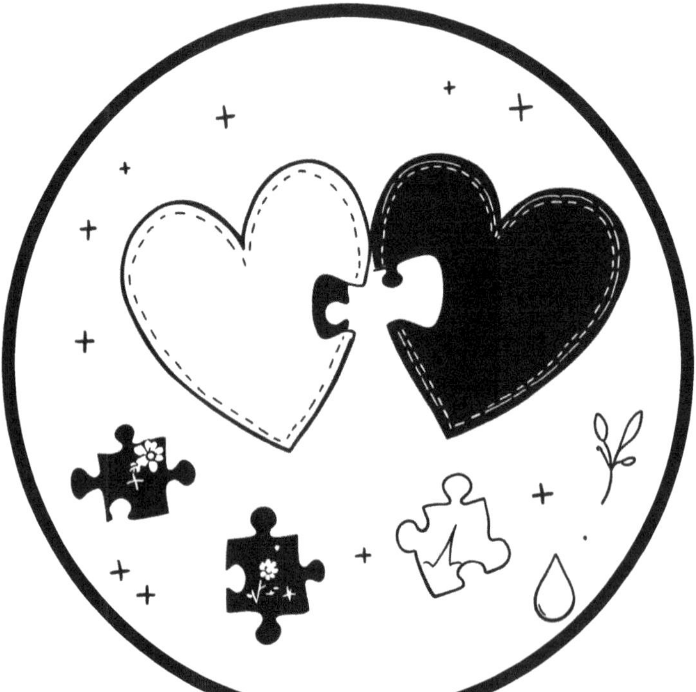

Unrequited Love = Mismatched Hearts

The pain I felt then
cut me like a knife.
But I hold no ill will
over heartbreak and strife.

It took years to heal
with countless tears cried,
and many loves lost
that just weren't right.

A repeated cycle
of mismatched hearts,
but each brought something new,
each played a part.

They shaped who I am,
helped me accept,
my tragic and giant heart -
for that, I'm blessed.

My heart now is hardy,
stronger each day,
and with each experience,
I let go of the pain.

I've forgiven all others,
forgiven myself too,
and chosen to love
my heart that stayed true.

Finding my heart
after being put through a blender,
pulp in a sieve,
but the pain is surrendered.

Reconstitute with water
from the depths of my soul,
reshape it anew,
let it set, make it whole.

Planting a seed
for love's flower to bloom,
waiting for magic
to lift me from gloom.

It takes time and patience,
but I know I'll find power,
to love myself truly,
and wait for that hour.

Unrequited Love = Mismatched Hearts – Reflection

"Unrequited Love = Mismatched Hearts" explores how even love that goes unreturned can leave a profound impact, shaping how we see ourselves and others. This poem suggests that unrequited love, though painful, offers valuable insights into self-worth and the courage it takes to let go of expectations. Sometimes, mismatched hearts reveal the strength in loving without expectation, guiding us toward a deeper acceptance of ourselves.

What can unrequited love teach you about loving yourself, even without validation from others? How might letting go of the need for reciprocation change how you choose to love?

READER NOTES:

THE WEIGHT

A great weight...
A great burden...
This thing called hate...
Some are good at locking it away...
Others wave it around on display...

How wonderful our world could be...
Could you foresee...
Not having all this hate...

But without it...
Would love seem so great?

THE WEIGHT - REFLECTION

Hate may seem like an unnecessary burden, but without it, could we truly recognize the warmth and light of love? "The Weight" explores the duality of love and hate, showing how each emotion, whether joyful or painful, contributes to the depth of our experiences. Accepting both sides of this duality helps us find harmony within ourselves, appreciating the contrasts that give life mcaning.

How do the challenges you face help you appreciate moments of peace, love, and joy? In what ways does embracing both positive and negative emotions bring a sense of balance to your life?

READER NOTES:

BOUND & FREE: A DUALITY

To Be Bound and gagged
All alone
Bleeding tears from my eyes
Who's in control?

You are not like me
I am not like you
Locked away forever
I am blind, deaf, and mute.

Alone.
No love, no touch, no compassion
Void of feeling, I cry.
Longing for expression.

Twisted images,
Flood my head.
Chaos incarnate,
Insomniac trends.

It would feel so good
To feel alive,
To drink in the blood of earth,
This thirst for life.

Darkness falls.
I am weak.
Paranoid, un-whole.
I dare not speak.

Wrapped in chains.
Writhing to be free.
Every twist feels...
Like razor blades to me.

Please release me.
Find the key.
Release me from my bondage.
Set my soul free…

BOUND & FREE: A DUALITY

To Be Free…

Along for the ride,
Not much else.
It is complicated -
Can't lose myself.

Deliver me,
Deliver me,
Deliver me.

Forgive me.

Please don't ask me
About my paranoid screams,
The sorrowful weeping,
And the lonely sighs of my dreams.

Where's my cloud and silver lining?
Where's the me
That's meant to release me
From the grave in which I'm dining?

BOUND & FREE: A DUALITY - REFLECTION

"Bound & Free" dives into the inner struggle between feeling trapped and the desperate yearning to break free. "Bound" portrays the pain of restriction, the torment of being held captive by our own fears, while "Free" speaks to the plea for release - a realization that freedom often lies within. Together, these pieces remind us that, even in the depths of captivity, the journey toward freedom may require us to be our own heroes, finding the courage to save ourselves when no one else can.

What parts of yourself still feel bound by past pain or fear? How might embracing both the desire for freedom and the challenge of self-rescue help you find your own path forward?

READER NOTES:

PERCEPTION & DECEPTION: THE DUALITY OF BEAUTY

Beauty is in the Eye

They say beauty is in the eye, but whose eyes count today?
Is it worth anything at all if it just fades away?
They say it's skin deep, but what does that mean?
Just shallow words on a glossy magazine.

Is it big breasts, a tiny waist, a pretty face?
Is it curves, poise, or how well you behave?
They tell me beauty is something within,
But it seems the world doesn't look past the skin.

A trick mirror's reflection that lies every day -
Telling me I'm not enough in its cruel display.
I don't need a mirror to know what I am,
But the world keeps reminding me of where I don't stand.

I know my worth, I know I'm fine,
But some days, I wish you'd cross that line -
Tell me I'm beautiful, just a time or two,
Let me hear it from the lips of you.

PERCEPTION & DECEPTION: THE DUALITY OF BEAUTY

Beauty's Façade

All the pretty words they said,
Were wrapped in lies instead.
Flattery fooled me once before,
Only later, did I know the score.

Now that I know it was all a ruse,
Trusting them left me battered and confused.
Now, whenever compliments I receive,
My instinct whispers, "They mean to deceive."

It doesn't matter how innocent they sound,
They twist my heart and turn it around.
The disbelief shows on my face -
They think me shameful, an utter disgrace.

"You look nice today" - I flinch and smile,
But behind every word, I fear their wiles.
The praises that once led me astray,
Echo and warn me to stay away.

Twisted, my sense of beauty and grace,
A gift now tarnished, a memory erased.
Like honeyed words that once tasted sweet,
Now bitterness lingers in every meet.

So many words that meant only harm,
Left every kindness raising alarm.
You think I doubt myself, my worth isn't seen -
But it's not me, it's the world I don't believe.

How tragic is it, to lose that trust,
To see darkness in what should be just?
To question the intentions behind kind eyes,
Believing love, warmth, and admiration are all a disguise.

PERCEPTION & DECEPTION: THE DUALITY OF BEAUTY - REFLECTION

"Perception & Deception" explores the longing to be truly seen for who we are, and the wounds left when admiration is only skin-deep. "Beauty is in the Eye" reflects the desire for genuine appreciation that goes beyond appearances, while "Beauty's Facade" reveals the disillusionment and distrust that arise when compliments turn to manipulation. These poems ask us to confront the impact of superficial judgments on our self-worth and invite us to find validation within rather than relying on others to define our value.

What has the experience of seeking validation taught you about self-worth? How might redefining beauty as more than appearance change the way you see yourself and others?

READER NOTES:

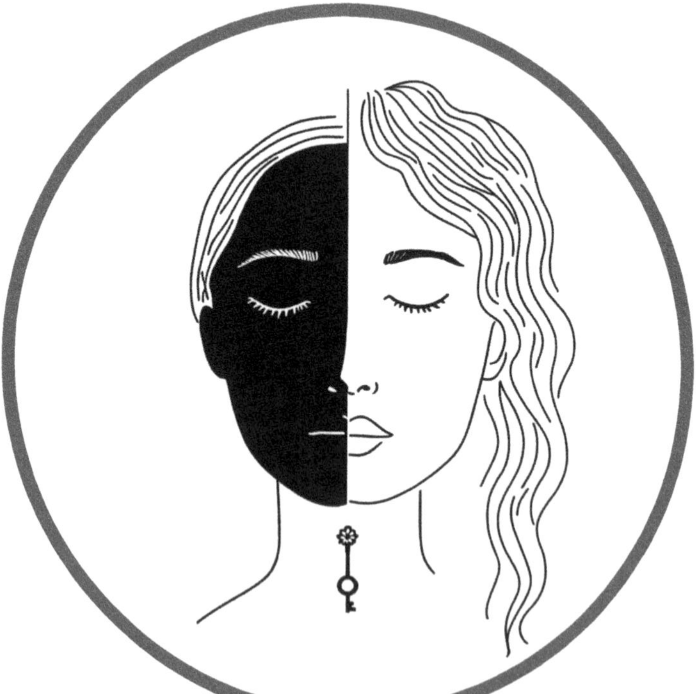

SELF-DECEPTION? SHIFT PERCEPTION

I'm not good enough.
I'm not pretty enough.
I'm not skinny enough.
I'm not cool enough.
I'm not smart enough.
I'm not happy enough.
I'm not wealthy enough.
I'll never be enough.
I'm okay, I'm alright, I'm fine!

No one will love me.
No one will care.
No one will help.
No one can understand.

I'm in this on my own.
This is the only way to survive.
What if tomorrow never comes?
I'm an empty shell inside.

These lies we tell ourselves.

When the truth is...
Even if we believe these things are true...

Only we can change ourselves.
And you are more than you realize.

You are good enough.
You are pretty enough.
You are skinny enough.
You are cool enough.
You are smart enough.
You are happy enough.
You are wealthy enough.
You are enough.
You are okay. You are alright. You are fine!

Someone does love you.
Someone does care.
Someone will help.
Someone can understand.

You're not on your own.
There are ways you can thrive
Focus on where you are today.
You are beautiful inside.

SELF-DECEPTION? SHIFT PERCEPTION - REFLECTION

"Self-Deception? Shift Perception" invites us to confront the lies we tell ourselves that can distort our sense of worth. Often, these beliefs take root unnoticed, shaping the way we see ourselves and the world. This poem encourages us to recognize the power of self-perception and the freedom that comes from challenging limiting beliefs.

What unkind beliefs about yourself are you ready to question? How might reframing your internal dialogue open up new possibilities for growth and self-acceptance?

READER NOTES:

IN SILENCE

Why don't you ever say anything?
Why don't we talk?
How about over dinner,
or while taking a walk?

                        Silence is deafening,
                        a heavy cloak we wear.
                        Words left unsaid
                        fill the room with despair.

The pauses stretch longer,
the distance grows wide.
What are we hiding,
what feelings denied?

                        Is it fear of conflict,
                        or fear of being wrong?
                        Is it safer to stay quiet,
                        than admit we don't belong?

In silence, the truth festers,
unspoken and unseen.
It grinds in the darkness,
like gears in a machine.

                        So, we sit in this stillness,
                        both knowing the cost,
                        of all that was unsaid,
                        and what we have lost.

IN SILENCE - REFLECTION

"In Silence" reflects the quiet distance that grows when words are left unsaid. While silence can sometimes shield us from conflict, it also builds walls that keep connection at bay. This poem invites us to explore the hidden costs of holding back and to consider the courage it takes to speak the truths that matter most.

What difficult conversations have you avoided, and how has that affected your relationships? How might embracing open dialogue - even when it's uncomfortable - strengthen your connections and bring you closer to understanding?

READER NOTES:

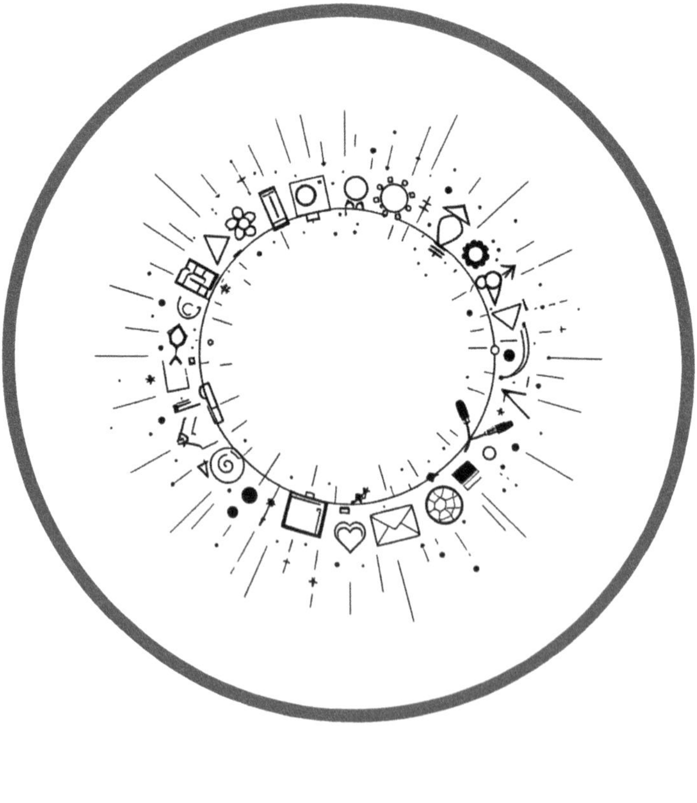

DIVERSITY THROUGH UNITY

I have been a victim
I have played the fool
I have come out swinging
I have kept my cool.

I have lost a fight
I have also won
I have cried myself to sleep
I have come undone.

I have rallied with allies
I have also walked away
The social justice warrior in me
simply couldn't stay.

I have lived on a sliver of hope
I have dared to dream
I have drifted high and low
I almost drowned in a steam.

I have felt others pain
I have heard the banshee cry
I have kept my heart open
Even when I wished I would die.

I have pushed buttons
Mine have been pushed too
Are things all that uncommon,
Between me and you?

Lend me your ears
I will tell you no lies
We have more in common
Than truth in disguise.

DIVERSITY THROUGH UNITY - REFLECTION

"Diversity Through Unity" reminds us that our struggles and strengths, though unique to each of us, are deeply connected. This poem speaks to the resilience and empathy that arise when we recognize our common humanity. Embracing both individuality and unity allows us to see ourselves reflected in others, bridging divides and deepening compassion.

How does acknowledging our shared struggles create a foundation for empathy? In what ways can celebrating both unity and diversity lead to a fuller understanding of ourselves and those around us?

READER NOTES:

HIDDEN IN PLAIN SIGHT

I kept my truths beneath the skin,
Buried deep, so none could win.
Layer by layer, I wove them tight,
Lost to shadows, hidden from sight.

I told myself I didn't need
To pull the thread or feel it bleed.
Yet whispers grew in the still of night,
Hints of truths that avoided light.

There's a comfort in the lies we keep,
A lullaby to help us sleep.
But every thread we fail to trace
Forms a knot we can't erase.

One day I paused, too tired to run,
Faced the threads I'd left undone.
In that tangled, twisted space,
I met myself and found my place.

Now each truth I dare to see,
Unwinds a part of what could be.
Hidden in plain sight, they wait,
Silent keys to unlock fate.

HIDDEN IN PLAIN SIGHT - REFLECTION

"Hidden in Plain Sight" invites us to uncover the truths we've kept buried, meeting ourselves in a raw, vulnerable state. This poem suggests that in facing the tangled threads of our hidden selves, we begin to understand our true place in life. By daring to look within, we reveal silent keys that may unlock new possibilities, helping us see not just who we are, but who we could become.

What parts of yourself have you kept hidden, and how might meeting them unfiltered bring clarity to your journey? In what ways can embracing both strengths and vulnerabilities help you unlock your own potential?

READER NOTES:

THE FEATHER'S WEIGHT: A SCRIBE'S TRUTH

I came to the place where shadows stretch long,
Where the wings of black unfurl - carrying purple's song.
A curtain of dusk, heavy as the silence I crave,
Folds me inward, deeper, into the underworld's grave.

Through the muck, the cold, the damp of this land,
I feel the earth's heartbeat pulse beneath my hand.
Time melts away, like film burning slow,
Each frame a lifetime, each echo a soul I know.

Empathy is a weight, a gift, a curse,
It presses the heart with joy and the grief of the universe.
I see the star-crossed fates, their love torn apart,
Feel the sting of loss, the fire of the heart.

Yet here, in the deep, I must weigh what is true,
Will the feather lift my spirit or bind me anew?
For Ma'at waits with her scales held high,
Asks not what I did, but why.

In the hall of two truths, where silence hums low,
The scribe stands, a witness to the heart's final show.
Before the scales, Ma'at's gaze sharp and wise,
Each deed arises - did I steal, did I lie?

Yet the question that lingers, deeper than sin,
Is not just what happened, but what stirred within.
For the heart may be light in the absence of blame,
But what of the shadows that whisper my name?

"I have not made others weep, nor caused them pain,
But did I stand idle as they suffered in vain?"
The scribe wonders, as the deeds blur and pass,
Through this tunnel of truths, reflections of glass.

Each step through the tunnel is colder, more still,
And each confession a mountain, a weight of the will.
"I have not stolen, nor spoken in haste,
But did I act out of love, or was it misplaced?"

Here, in the cavern where time melts away,
The heart and the feather begin their display.
The deeds of a lifetime etched in the air,
Do they free me or bind me - do I dare to compare?

The cold of the tunnel, heavy and vast,
Begins to release, as the shadows fade past.
Each step I take, from the weight of the scales,
Carries the truth of my heart, as it prevails.

The light in the distance, a promise reborn,
Beckons me forward, away from the scorn.

Through the veil of the past, I rise, and I see,
That the darkness was never the enemy of me.

For in the descent, I found what was true,
Not just the deeds done, but the heart that grew.
The feather, once feared, now rests in my hand,
A symbol of balance, of all that I am.

Out of the muck, out of the cold,
I step toward the sun, toward the stories untold.
Ma'at's gaze softens, her judgment now clear,
It was never just fear that brought me here.

From the black wings of descent to purple skies wide,
I rise into day, with truth by my side.
The journey continues, but this chapter's complete,
The scribe ascends, with the ground beneath my feet.

THE FEATHER'S WEIGHT: A SCRIBE'S TRUTH - REFLECTION

"The Feather's Weight" invites us into a moment of self-reckoning, drawing on the symbol of Ma'at - a goddess in ancient Egyptian mythology who represents truth, balance, and moral integrity. In this journey, the heart is weighed against a feather, asking us not only what we've done but why we've done it. This poem explores the difficult process of examining our intentions alongside our actions, urging us to confront both empathy and guilt, light and shadow, to find a deeper sense of balance and self-acceptance.

How can weighing your intentions with your actions help you grow? In what ways does acknowledging both your light and shadow bring a fuller understanding of yourself?

READER NOTES:

PARADOX: CERTAINTY & DOUBT

I once thought certainty was the only way,
A solid ground where truth could stay.
But life whispered doubts, quiet yet clear,
A shadowed presence, always near.

Certainty promised a sense of peace,
Yet left me trapped, afraid to release
The grip on things I thought I knew,
While doubt crept in, bold and true.

Doubt told me to question, to pause,
To seek the "why" beneath each cause.
It felt like betrayal, to loosen my grip,
But doubt held my hand, a steadying slip.

In this paradox, I found a path -
A middle ground, neither fear nor wrath.
Certainty and doubt, woven tight,
Each giving depth to wrong and right.

Now I trust what I can't always see,
Holding both certainty and mystery.
For truth, I learned, can shift and sway,
Yet still be whole, in its own way.

PARADOX: CERTAINTY & DOUBT - REFLECTION

"Paradox: Certainty & Doubt" invites us to confront the discomfort of not having all the answers. It highlights that both certainty and doubt have value - certainty gives us direction, while doubt keeps us open to new insights. This tension, rather than being something to resolve, can be embraced as a part of our complex truths. Allowing ourselves to sit with this paradox fosters a resilient kind of wisdom, one that evolves with each experience.

How can embracing both certainty and doubt help you navigate life's uncertainties? In what ways does questioning your beliefs deepen your understanding of yourself and your values? What might it look like to trust in a truth that can shift and change, knowing it's part of a larger journey?

READER NOTES:

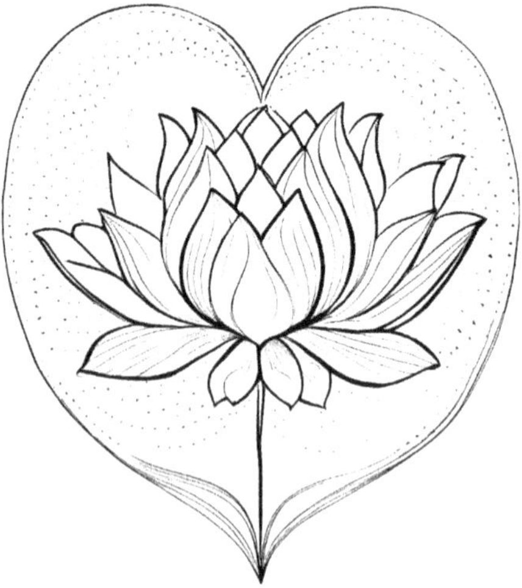

ABOUT THE AUTHOR

Melissa, also known as Mo Jo Jo, is a writer, poet, and conversationalist who celebrates the paradoxes within herself. An introvert with a deep curiosity about people, she values meaningful connections and often finds inspiration in unexpected conversations with strangers.

After a 17-year break from writing, Melissa returned to the page, rekindling her passion through a journey that explored both shadow and light. She writes for those navigating their own winding paths, hoping her words offer a sense of connection and a reminder that life, in all its messiness, is worth embracing.

Beyond writing, Melissa finds joy in painting, music, movies, theater, and culinary exploration - creative outlets that add depth to her journey and keep her work authentic.

Upcoming Projects from Mo Jo Jo:

Poetry of Everyday Tao: Untangling the Mind on a Creative Path (a poetry and art collection)

Timeless Echoes (a fiction)

Sowing Flowers in Grave Dirt (an auto-fiction)

My Dear Friend & The Pig Butcher (a novel - working title)

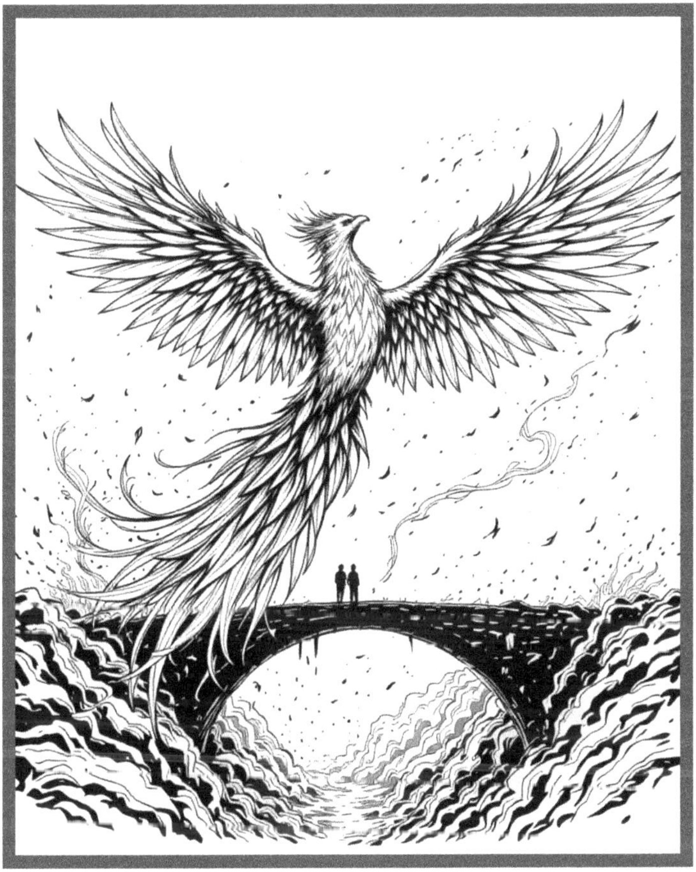